The Water Vole Book

by Hugh Warwick

Series editor Jane Russ

Dedication

To our rivers – we must not let greed
destroy these ribbons of life.

Contents

The Water Vole

It might be easy to dismiss this small rodent –
people often do. However, the water vole is worthy
of attention; unfortunately, the attention it receives
is due to it having one of the most rapid and serious
population declines of any British wild mammal.
This bundle of brown fur is many things: it is a
measure of the quality of our landscape; it is food for
many predators; it is definitely cute, and it is woven
into the fabric of our favourite stories. So it's worth
looking after, and the book you're about to read will
tell you why.

What is a Water Vole?

What is a Water Vole?

Water voles are rodents. While they are of a similar size to the brown rat they are in many respects more like mini-beavers, without the flattened tail or the dam building.

Though there is some evidence that they are, on a slightly smaller scale, ecosystem engineers just like their bigger cousins! The tunnels they excavate in river banks, using those sharp, rodent teeth, along with their habit of grazing alongside their paths and creating small lawns near their burrows, all help increase the diversity of riparian life – our watersides are a lesser place without water voles.

Differentiating them from rats is a bit trickier. If you do get a chance, even a glance should help define which species you have seen. The water vole has a more rounded and 'chubby' face and is altogether more cute, despite the orange teeth, coloured by the iron in the enamel that keeps them sharp. Rats have upright, visible pink ears, longer tails, pointed faces and, if you get close enough, bare feet. Water voles have furry paws and their ears are small and hidden.

A very clear difference comes when you disturb them, which is the most likely way with an accidental observation. If they are in the water, rats will carry on swimming away, but the water vole does a dive, generating a distinctive 'plop' sound.

Additionally, whilst rats keep just their head in the air, water voles are more buoyant, so swim with more of their body exposed above the surface. Whilst they are adept at swimming, they do not have webbed feet and do not use their tail as a rudder, relying on doggy paddle. They are well-furred, having the same insulating style as beavers and otters, with long, silky guard-hairs and short, wavy underhairs, however, they do not have the same sort of resistance to water.

With prolonged submergence the fur becomes waterlogged, leading to hypothermia if the vole cannot find dry land.

Their bodies are 14-22cm long and the tail 9-14cm and they weigh between 150-300g, making them slightly smaller than the brown rat. However, they are the largest vole in Britain. Our other voles are the bank vole (*Myodes glareolus*), which pitches in at up to 40g, and the field vole (*Microtus agrestis*) which is of similar size but differentiated from the bank vole by relative tail length and fur colour. Bank voles tend to be more reddish and russet, field voles more yellowy grey. A water vole's tail is 60% of head and body; a bank vole's tail is 50% and a field vole just 30%. The final relative is the Orkney vole, which is, unsurprisingly, found on Orkney. It is also larger, weighing up to 52g but is also not originally from Orkney. To add to the mystery, the Orkney vole was introduced from continental Europe over 5000 years ago, where it is known as the common vole (*Microtus arvalis*).

Fossil evidence shows that there have been other water voles in Britain. Back in the Pliocene and Early Pleistocene, around 3-2 million years ago, there were at least four different species in a range of sizes. None of them are still around today. There is a soft cliff on the north Norfolk coast near West Runton that has yielded amazing mammal fossils, laid down in what is known as the Cromerian stage, around half a million years ago. Here has been found *Arvicola cantiana*, a direct ancestor of our water vole. The first record for *Arvicola amphibius*, the vole we are concentrating on in this book, is from the Tornewton Cave in Devon and dates back around 30,000 years.

There are no water vole remains to be found from the last ice age, around 20,000 years ago, when glaciers reached down to the Midlands, as the parts of Britain not under ice were a bleak tundra environment. However, as the retreat of ice picked up pace, around 10,000 years ago, they returned and have been a familiar component of our landscape ever since.

Though water voles tend to be brown, this is not an absolute. The water voles of north and north-west Scotland tend to be black (melanic) and a study in Wester Ross revealed that 70% were black, 20% brown and rather delightfully, 10% were described as 'black and tan'. Melanic voles are not restricted to Scotland and have been reported from most counties in Britain. Common with all mammals, water voles can also come dressed in various pale forms from leucistic and flavistic (light brown and golden brown respectively) to the true albinos, complete with pink eyes.

What is in a name?

Taxonomists create names that are nested within a hierarchical structure so for the water vole you start with the kingdom, which is animal (as opposed to plant, fungi, bacteria). The phylum is Chordata; they are vertebrates with a backbone. The class is mammal, differentiating it from fish, birds, reptiles and amphibians. The order is Rodentia, with rodents defined in large part by their teeth and their need to gnaw to wear down a single pair of continuously growing incisors in each of the upper and lower jaws. Their family is *Cricetidae*; which includes hamsters, voles and lemmings. The genus (now we are getting into the nitty-gritty) is *Arvicola* and the species is *amphibius*, which gives us the binomial *Arvicola amphibius*.

These binomials are important as people call organisms by all sorts of local names, which can lead to confusion. Having one centrally agreed system means ecologists from all over the world can understand one another. For example, it is possible to hear someone talking about a water vole and find that they are referring to something quite different, as there is an animal going by that name in the northwestern United States and southern Canada. *Microtus richardsoni* was historically considered to be a member of the genus *Arvicola* but genetics has revealed it to be more closely related to the *Microtus* branch of the family.

The largest vole in North America, *Microtus richardsoni* is smaller than our version, measuring in at up to 150g. They are easily identified among the small rodents of the Americas by their particularly large rear feet, which are up to 34mm in length, enabling them to move at a considerable speed in water.

'Our' water vole has gone through something of a reinvention. It was not until 2005 that the International Code for Zoological Nomenclature (ICZN) decided on the species, *amphibius*. Up until that time the accepted naming for the water vole was *Arivcola terrestris*, somewhat at odds with its rather more aquatic common name.

Water voles have come by other names too, most famously as the water rat, 'Ratty' of *The Wind in the Willows* fame. And while those who read Kenneth Grahame's masterpiece will forever be inclined towards a love for the rodent, the 'rat' bit of the name, along with the fact that they are similar in appearance if you get only a brief view, has not helped them in the great battle for attention among the public.

Despite the name change, there are some rather terrestrial water voles in Britain. The ecologist Peter Cooper reported on these very interesting rodents in the magazine *British Wildlife* in June 2021. The story began with a report in 2008 from a Glasgow housing estate of a 'rat' problem. When checked, the rats were found to be water voles, living quite happily half a kilometre from the nearest water source.

Remarkably, this population now constitutes one of the highest densities in the UK with around 100-156 per hectare, compared to a healthy reedbed, which can cope with 40-50/ha.

So how unusual is this? Well, consider the name that got changed. This is a vole that has a fossorial, or burrowing, lifestyle across Europe. And while the UK is trying hard to get them back to healthy numbers, there are places on the continent where they can reach such densities that they can become significant pests.

There is historical evidence for the presence of water voles well away from water and it has been suggested that the rodent used to fill the niche taken over by the rabbit, which did not make Britain its home until the time of the Romans.

Good evidence for the historical distribution and, to some extent, density of many species of wild animal can be found within parish records, most amazingly collected together by Roger Lovegrove in his book *Silent Fields*. However, for water voles there is a problem. They are difficult to disentangle from rats; for example, Lovegrove reports that over 135,000 'rats' were killed over 35 years in the 18th century and handed in to the Dorset parish of Sherborne.

Yet brown rats only arrived in Britain in 1730 and black rats tend not to make their homes so far inland, so the most likely species to have suffered in such a way are water voles.

Peter Cooper's 2021 research reveals that historical fossorial behaviour was not the norm, to such an extent that it was noted by naturalists such as Gilbert White as unusual behaviour. There is some evidence of their beaver-like form emerging in beaver-like behaviour. No, a little water vole is not going to be felling a large tree, but they have been reported as pests of tree nurseries, where their crime was to bite through roots of willow, poplar and apple, up to 7cm thick.

But for now, the Glasgow voles are something of an anomaly.

What Do Water Voles Eat?

What Do Water Voles Eat?

This question was famously, if erroneously, answered by Kenneth Grahame, where Ratty's luncheon-basket contained 'cold chicken... cold tonguecoldhamcoldbeefpickledgherkinssalad-frenchrollscressandwiches pottedmeatgingerbeerlemonadesoda water...'

While *The Wind in the Willows* may contain some of the most luminous writing about the river – 'this sleek, sinuous, full-bodied animal, chasing and chuckling, gripping things with a gurgle and leaving them with a laugh...' – it is entirely not to be trusted as a guide to rudimentary natural history. It is likely that a water vole would avail themselves of just the salad and the cress should one stumble across such a picnic.

If the real diet of the water vole was to be written in the style of Kenneth Grahame it would be just too long.

They are herbivorous, feeding on riparian vegetation and eating an awful lot of it, consuming up to 80% of their bodyweight a day. There are stories of them consuming far greater quantities; for example, a 285g male seemed to consume 2kg of fruit, though in reality a lot of this would have been stored away underground – otherwise he would have popped!

So much of what we know about water vole food preferences comes from Rob Strachan's groundbreaking national survey of 1989-90, during which he travelled the country in a camper van recording activity at nearly 3,000 sites. The analysis of food remains found that water voles were feeding on 227 species of plant, and those were just the bits he could readily identify.

The most frequently eaten plants are grasses, rushes and sedge. These, along with other local delights, will often be consumed at a feeding station – areas along their commonly used paths on which the vole will sit and prepare their food. Yes, they do food preparation; cutting long stems of plants into manageable 8-10cm pieces, usually with a distinctive 45-degree angle (a small collection of these will be returned to the home nest for consumption). Feeding stations are also useful for the field ecologist as they provide not just evidence of the presence of water voles but also give an insight into what they are consuming.

The cut stems and the lawns both give credence to the thought of water voles as mini-beavers, though of course, the beavers are 100 times the size and leave not stems of vegetation, but branches.

Their diet is dictated in large part by location and by season. While in the early spring they gnaw bark, and eat nettles and grass, in the summer they will tend to go for the rich growth of willowherb, watercress and branched bur-reed. By the autumn they will seek out windfall apples with their excellent sense of smell, climb brambles to eat blackberries and will then begin to feast on hawthorn berries to pack on weight before winter, when the focus shifts underground to roots, rhizomes and bulbs.

While they are almost exclusively vegan in their choice of food, females will tend to lapse while pregnant and start to include invertebrates such as caddisflies, snails, small fish and crayfish in her diet.

Best-selling author Kate Long has studied her local colony of water voles since moving to Whitchurch, Shropshire in 1990. Such close amateur observation has given her a level of insight into their world that rivals any 'proper' scientist. She has found that the food of choice is apple, preferably overripe and kept moist in a small plastic bag in her pocket. She picks it out with litter pickers to avoid any of her scent getting onto the fruit before placing it beside the small brook that runs near her home. Within minutes, bright, beady eyes appear, drawn to the burrow entrance by their sensitive nose. Sometimes the vole will grab and run, but more often they will sit and eat. It is one of the most charming aspects of the water vole that they can be quite visible while they snack, and that they do it in a manner which is utterly endearing, sitting on their haunches while dextrous front paws hold food in a very human manner.

For Kate Long it was spotting a water vole when she was just eight years old that gave her a life-long passion. Now, after studying the decline of these beautiful native mammals over the past few decades, she understands more than ever the urgent need to preserve the habitat and vital wildlife corridors they need.

Since 2006 she has maintained a detailed record of water voles and other wildlife she sees on her blog, giving an amazing insight into what can be seen if we take the trouble to observe quietly, sitting and waiting and occasionally luring with apple!

Spotting water voles is an important part of study but, like many mammals, it is often through indirect means that their presence can be seen. Water voles have a very distinctive

way of depositing faeces; they create latrines throughout their territory, in particular at either end, on which droppings accumulate over time, gifting researchers an indicator of their presence.

No other small mammal creates droppings like that of the water vole. The best way to describe them is as a 'tic-tac' shape, 8-12mm long, 4-5mm thick, often close to water and, while variable in colour, usually dark green when broken up. Making the life of an ecologist just that bit better, the droppings tend to be odourless, at least to the ecologist, as these latrines are also key messaging posts. Any previous droppings will be stamped on by the vole, who also swipes their leg across their flank where a scent gland exudes an oily orange substance that provides added detail to the deposit. The information shared is likely to include the sex, breeding condition and fitness of the depositor. It is also possible that anyone paying attention to the latrine would also get an indication of the quality of the food to be found in the next stretch of bank.

This information has a very important role to play in water vole life. Most water voles live along linear waterways and when a vole has found a good patch it likes to keep it to itself, though this is more applicable to females than males. Very roughly speaking, females have territories that they defend while males have home ranges across which they roam.

There is a broader picture to the water vole's patch – they have a sort of colonial social system in place. Rob Strachan described this as being like a string of sausages along a waterway.

The linear colonies are not completely isolated, and there has been growing awareness of the importance of the metapopulation, that is the wider population within an area and the patches to which and from which water voles will move. Saving a single stretch of river for voles is not going to be enough to sustain a viable population if there is no way for these voles to link in with wider vole communities. There needs to be space for young to move when they disperse and opportunities to have a system replenished should flood, disease or predation cause a big drop off in numbers.

Water Vole
Life and Death

The Vole Year

Water voles don't hibernate; they are around over winter but they are not very visible. Most of their time is spent in their burrow system where they store food.

They also use the burrows to find food, eating roots of plants from below. They will feed above the surface, but usually only when vegetation is dense and they can create runs, keeping well under cover. Interestingly, territoriality breaks down over winter and from December voles can be found to nest communally. This brings obvious benefits in terms of extra warmth.

Spring starts early, or at least water vole behaviour does, with the females forcing the changes as their hormones kick in and they retreat to their separate patches of river bank. The latrines come back into business as signalling posts, males start to pay more attention, and any space along the stretch will get filled up either with expanded ranges or migration from further afield. If there are the voles around that is.

Mating usually starts in April, with peak numbers of young emerging in April and May after a 22-day-long gestation. The average number of young is five, and the female is ready to mate again within a few days of birth. The most recorded litters within one year is five, and while this might seem like an extraordinary number of voles to be appearing, as

you will learn, the threats they face mean they need all the recruitment they can get.

By June the youngsters are out. Having spent around 25 days in the nest they are strong enough to enter the water but do not have the swimming capacity of the adults. That is not to say they are at risk of drowning, more that they tend to bob around like corks on the surface.

High summer sees the beginning of vole politics as the population grows and dispersals start to take place. Juvenile males and females with lower ranking are encouraged to seek their fortune elsewhere. The dominant females will start out settling within their mother's territory, and may even usurp them when population pressures are too great.

Peak vole is in September. It is possible that some of the first litter females in the year will have started to breed by July and may themselves manage a second litter in their first year. Given the threats they face from hungry carnivores, it is a good job they can reproduce quickly when the conditions allow. As autumn arrives, dispersal increases and there is general preparation for winter. Hormone levels subside, sexual activity stops and a more communal air allows the voles to rub along beside each other, collecting food to store underground.

While water voles don't hibernate, when the weather is particularly bad they can enter what is known as torpor, a state somewhere between sleep and hibernation. Periods of activity occur sporadically throughout the rest of the winter before the whole cycle starts again.

Water voles are often mistaken for brown rats but, as you have now learned, there are easy ways to tell them apart.

Now, everyone loves water voles, which is why it is fortunate they are able to reproduce quite quickly, because 'love' in this sense is from the perspective of potential predators, as it feels like everyone is out to get them. Water voles are apparently very tasty and they form an important part of the diet of many. Among the enemies these bundles of fur have to avoid are the fox, otter, grass snake, stoat, weasel, brown rat, owls, heron and pike.

This was one of the more accurate observations in *The Wind in the Willows*, as Ratty says, 'Weasels – and stoats – and foxes – and so on [...] well, you can't really trust them, and that's the fact.'

Owl pellets (regurgitated fur and bone) are a fantastic way of working out what has been eaten, and studies have shown that in some areas up to 30% of the diet of barn and short-eared owls has been water vole. The presence of water vole bones in the pellets around golden eagle nests also provides evidence of them in parts of the Highlands of Scotland that might not be surveyed very often.

Water voles are often mistaken for brown rats but, as you have now learned, there are easy ways to tell them apart. Brown rats can also be predators of water voles, in particular taking those in nests or young just out, and if rat numbers reach high levels they can also displace water voles from their territories. Research has shown that when rats are present in high numbers water voles will change their behaviour, foraging more in the late afternoon and evening and after sunrise. When no rats are present they tend to be active throughout the night at roughly three-hourly intervals.

For small land predators, such as stoats and weasels, and airborne threats such as owls, the water vole has the water and will swiftly scamper to the nearest source and disappear. To deter waterborne predators they will kick up sediment as they dive and swim and make for their burrows, and the burrow network also provides sanctuary from bigger threats, like foxes, so whilst the water vole is eaten by many things it has evolved a strategy that keeps it going, just. Until things change too rapidly.

Mink and Other Threats

The passion for fur coats had an appalling impact on the lives of countless mink, fox, ermine, beaver and otter, to name but a few. It still does in parts of the world where the captive breeding of these animals continues. Thankfully there is a societal move to retire this cruel trade to the same bin of history as badger-baiting and fox hunting. Fortunately for the water vole, they seem to have been overlooked despite a good deal of fluff on their bodies.

Rob Strachan believed it was their small size which let them off the hook but recorded that, 'one Victorian naturalist with the grand name of Heneage Cocks did make a small fireside rug out of water vole skins collected from the River Thames, near Marlow.'

The threat to water voles from the fur industry was never going to be their own desirability. No, there is one animal that has had an enormously dramatic impact on British ecosystems: the American mink. The fur of this amazing creature is both luxuriant and water repellent which, together with their partially webbed feet, makes them a brilliant predator superbly adapted to a semi-aquatic riparian lifestyle.

Mink first arrived in the UK in 1929 but were largely restricted to fur farms, though escapees were noted from the 1930s. These became established, and the first breeding mink in the wild were recorded in 1956. When the fur trade in the UK was coming to an end, some fur farms decided to capitalise on the poorly thought through protests of some animal rights activists, who were seeking the release of caged animals.

Mink swimming

It is especially damaging for a colony of voles if a female mink settles into their patch and breeds, because the demands of baby mink are easily met by vulnerable voles.

They were able to dispose of their victims in a manner which generated an insurance handout, handing on the blame to the activists who by then were aware that such actions were not beneficial to the wider environment.

In 1995 there were estimated to be over 100,000 mink in the UK and they have been responsible for serious damage to the breeding success of some ground-nesting birds. However, they have caused a particular problem for the water vole.

Mink are a particularly effective predator of the water vole, especially female mink who, unlike the larger male, are able to fit into the burrows of the vole. Because they are also very adept in the water, the usual escape techniques that have served the water vole well over the millennia are rendered useless. It is especially damaging for a colony of voles if a female mink settles into their patch and breeds, because the demands of baby mink are easily met by vunerable voles.

To give you an indication of the effectiveness of mink at causing havoc, consider this example from the extremely valuable, but quite technical, *Water Vole Conservation Handbook*. Along a 4km stretch of the Wendover Arm of the Grand Union Canal in Buckinghamshire there were over 120 water voles in 2001. The population had been there for at least 80 years and was being monitored during the breeding season.

It is not mink alone that have caused the dramatic declines in water voles. In fact, they were already suffering before mink were widespread.

Mink arrived in September 2001 and between then and April 2002 all but one individual had been removed.

It is not mink alone that have caused the dramatic declines in water voles. In fact they were already suffering before mink were widespread. We have lost around 90% of our wetland habitat in the last 100 years through the combination of extensive drainage, unsustainable farming and development, urbanisation and abstraction. Drainage to 'improve' the land is an obvious threat as it removes water vole habitat. Farming is a particular problem when livestock are allowed to over-graze the riparian vegetation and trample the banks. Taking arable cultivation right to the edge of the waterway not only removes water vole food but increases the amount of agrotoxin runoff. Attempts to control flooding of farmland and suburbia have led to the canalising of ditches and streams coupled to unsympathetic dredging regimes, this is known as 'radical linearalization.' Add to this the reinforcement of banks with concrete and metal and, well, it's easy to see how the water vole has had it hard.

Perhaps unexpectedly, flooding is a real problem for water voles. Yes, they can swim, but if their burrows are inundated then they are lost, no longer a bolt-hole, no longer a safe place to raise young. Our weather is being affected by a changing climate, and as flooding becomes more common so the voles will find their homes destroyed more often.

The toxic runoff into waterways is interesting. It is hard to find clear evidence of a direct impact because the work of exposing water voles to the complex cocktails that seep into their home has never been done and will not be. It would be a brave advocate of industrial agriculture that claimed there was no impact from the heady mix of the herbicide, glyphosate, numerous insecticides, fungicides and growth promoters, all of this coupled with the runoff from livestock effluent massively increasing nitrate and phosphate levels in the once crystal streams and rivers of the UK.

Water voles exist as a colony, which in turn is part of a metapopulation, a wider population that is proximate enough by to be able to share dispersing young and fill voids should they appear.

Another factor is the fragmentation of water vole habitats. Alongside the loss of so much waterside world, there is the bigger problem of the remaining bits that are still good for water voles becoming isolated. Water voles exist as a colony, which in turn is part of a metapopulation, a wider population that is proximate enough to be able to share dispersing young and fill voids should they appear. If the colony becomes isolated and is hit by predators, flooding or pollution, then it becomes difficult for new voles to take over and you end up with a local extinction.

Now add into the mix a new and dramatic threat, the mink, and it is not hard to see how 'ratty' has vanished from 97% of its former range and has a population some 98% down on peak vole.

And research is revealing one further threat. While it has long been recognised that pet and feral cats are a serious threat to many birds and mammals, dogs have had a somewhat better press. However, experiments that have excluded dogs from riverbanks using fencing have shown a marked increase in water vole presence when dogs are kept away.

All of these threats mean that water voles are now benefiting from some considerable protection in the UK. They were added to Schedule 5 of the Wildlife and Countryside Act in 2008, which prohibits killing, injuring, taking or possessing, selling or buying water voles.

Which is good, but what is better is the prohibition of damage or extra damage, destruction of places used by water voles as shelter.

Natural England can issue a licence allowing for these rules to be broken. Which may seem like a strange thing to offer, but it is important. Especially for people like Derek Gow.

Water Vole Reintroductions

When a population of water voles has been exterminated by the combined agencies of industrialised agriculture and cunning carnivores, there are two possible reactions. One would be to let 'nature take its course', despite it very much not being nature that took us to that point in the first place, and hope that water voles find their way back to that particular stretch of water. The other is to do something, which is where Derek Gow comes into the story.

Derek Gow has more recently made his name breeding and releasing beavers at his Coombeshead Farm just north of Dartmoor, which is actually much less of a farm now than it was when he arrived. Today it is a rewilding initiative spread over 60 hectares (for the time being) and he has already shown what dramatic changes can be achieved in a very short space of time. Biodiversity and bioabundance has rocketed as livestock have been removed. Income is secured in large part by his beautiful and highly successful tourism venture – people want to come and see what a landscape which has been given back some of its freedom can look like. They come because they want a glimpse of hope.

The journey for Derek started out from his ecological consultancy work with water voles. Over the last 22 years he has bred and released around 27,000 of these wonderful animals.

A healthy mix of vegetation, fruit and vegetables is fed to the couples while they are left to do what small mammals do best.

He has got the process of vole breeding down to a fine art. There is an extensive outdoor area where, each March, one male and one female are put into secure enclosures. They try and choose larger males, because the females can be quite feisty. A healthy mix of vegetation, fruit and vegetables is fed to the couples while they are left to do what small mammals do best. By the end of July, it is time to do the first check and all youngsters weighing over 100g are collected up and got ready for release into the wild. The breeding pairs get their moment in the wild in August and September.

November is when the outdoor pens get emptied out and the remaining voles either brought into the vole room or left to be put back into breeding pairs outside. This system ensures there is a cycle of voles and is necessary, as even in these cosseted conditions they only live for between 12-18 months. In the wild the average lifespan of a water vole is just five months.

Perhaps surprisingly, one of the most important tools of the trade is the outer packet carton of Pringles, empty and washed. These reconstituted potato snacks come in a container that has the dimensions of a water vole burrow, meaning a skilled operative, and there are plenty that Derek has trained, can easily collect a vole for its weekly check-up in the vole room.

First the vole is coaxed from its smaller cage into a large box, then the crisp container is placed alongside it, offering a bolthole to the startled rodent. The bolthole is then picked up and the vole encouraged to emerge. As soon as it does, its tail is firmly grasped and the animal can be given a visual check.

These are important voles, the future of their species, so health is checked. The vole is allowed to slip back into its burrow before the container is then weighed with a spring balance, Derek must make sure these beauties are of a good weight. While this is happening their cages are being cleared out and replenished with food – and what food they get. The staff may be animal handlers, but they are also in training for a role as a commis chef with the many apples and carrots they have had to slice and dice.

Breeding water voles is not all that has to be done, of course. There is no point reintroducing water voles if the mink that wiped them out are just waiting to have the table replenished. Adding water voles to the sink hole of a poor-quality river will not lead to a successful return of this charismatic animal either.

Breeding water voles is not all that has to be done, of course. There is no point reintroducing water voles if the mink that wiped them out are just waiting to have the table replenished.

This is something that requires more work; the causes behind the decline in water voles need to be reversed. If there is no mink control, the water voles will not be able to return. If the banks of rivers are maintained in a linear fashion, something that some might consider to be neat and tidy but others look upon as glorified canals, the voles will not settle into a new home. If livestock are allowed to graze to the water's edge, ratty will stay away. Furthermore, if a new release of water voles takes place in isolation, without the possibility of connecting up with other groups, there could be a genetic effect, reducing their vigour and posing a risk to the lives of those that do go exploring further afield.

Each of these points needs addressing. Mink control is the most pressing concern, and for some the most morally challenging. Should we kill one wild animal to help another? For example, hedgehogs were being killed on the Uists in the Outer Hebrides for four years from 2003 because they were accused of eating the eggs of ground-nesting birds. These wading birds were considered more valuable than the hedgehogs because the hedgehogs were a recent import, a few having been introduced in the early 1970s. The killing continued until research proved that it was unnecessary and the hedgehogs could simply be moved to the mainland.

The Game and Wildlife Conservation Trust developed a very effective 'mink raft' that allows footprints and scat to be recorded.

At the same time in New Zealand hedgehogs, again an import – this time from the late 19th century – were being killed due to their conservation impact on native species. In this instance there is far less complaint as there is no alternative available.

So for the mink, they could be rounded up and housed in a mink zoo until they died of old age. This, of course, is absurd and would be massively cruel. Fantasy contraception has been thought of as a solution, but by the time this worked at a population level, if it ever could work, the water voles would have been removed from the countryside. The alternative is to catch the mink in cages and kill them as humanely as possible.

Dark-humoured conservationists have even mooted the idea of creating a supply of 'ethical' mink fur products from the results of the campaign to remove them from the country.

Mink control is not entered into lightly. Conservationists do not, on the whole, enjoy killing things, because when we talk of control, that is just the sanitised way of saying that they are being killed. To kill a mink, you need to catch a mink and to catch one you need to know where the mink are active. The Game and Wildlife Conservation Trust developed a very effective 'mink raft' that allows footprints and scat to be recorded. This is important because mink may range over 5km of riverbank.

When a mink is caught it is illegal to release it back into the wild. It has to be killed.

Once the presence of mink is confirmed the raft can be converted from tracking station to live trap. When a mink is caught it is illegal to release it back into the wild. It has to be killed and the best legal way to do that is with a high-powered air pistol or rifle.

Technology is also stepping in and the arrival of 'smart rafts' is proving to be a game changer. These rafts have an additional unit attached which sends a message to a mobile phone when the door of the trap is triggered. This does away with the tracking component of the pro-cess, meaning they can be deployed permanently in trapping mode, thereby picking up transient mink moving through the wider landscape, animals that would be long gone by the time the old tracking rafts were checked and a trap installed. The message sent to the trap controller means that animal welfare is improved. Yes, the mink will still meet the same fate, but the time spent in the trap can be significantly reduced which in turn reduces the distress felt by the captive animal. This also means that any accidental capture of other animals, 'bycatch', can be released sooner.

The rafts, both smart and 'dumb', are a good start but for really successful mink control there needs to be wider landscape view which is hard to achieve. Fortunately, ecologist Dr Merryl Gelling is developing an online application that allows data to be collected from the many individual control projects across the country.

This in turn will help create more detailed maps, identifying mink control hotspots which can be extended and ideally linked together throughout catchments and landscapes.

A case study from the River Deben in Suffolk gives an insight into how effective water vole recovery plans can be. The Suffolk Wildlife Trust carried out a baseline survey in 1997 and found that nearly 80% of sites along 15km of river were occupied by water voles. By 2003 a repeat survey revealed that less than 50% of sites showed evidence of water voles, and there was widespread evidence of mink. A water vole recovery plan was initiated and the first step was to remove mink. Over three years 101 were killed. And the result? Well, the result should not be measured in dead mink but in the fact that the next survey showed voles back in 80% of the sites along the river.

This was not all that was done to ensure the recovery of the water vole population. Mink control was also undertaken in parallel with habitat enhancement work. We now know that while mink may be the obvious threat to water voles, the voles were were being massively impacted before these carnivores started carving up the remaining habitats.

How do we repair a riparian habitat? The much-missed Rob Strachan wrote that the guidance 'should be written after 10 years of solid practical and scientific research' but that 'to do nothing until we have such information may mean we are too late'. This is a real indication of the urgency felt by the people who could see what was happening.

First and foremost we need to protect existing habitats, periodically fencing off the reed and sedge beds and the herb-rich grassland along the water's edge. This will reduce livestock grazing, leave more food and cover for the voles and protect their burrows from being damaged by the hoofs of heifers above, compacting the soil. This can be especially effective if the stream or river has been allowed to meander as a pocket of habitat can be secured with minimal fencing. There needs to be occasional grazing to prevent the riparian strip turning to woodland, which is not so good for voles.

There are some waterways which have habitually been managed to within an inch of their lives. When 'weed' cutting, in order to save costs contractors will be brought in for a minimal amount of time to cover as much of this water-edge habitat as possible. Removing many kilometres of habitat in one fell swoop will seriously reduce the ability of water voles to thrive. Cutting back can be done sympathetically, leaving a mosaic of habitats and achieving a degree of tidiness and control. This is done by leaving one bank unmolested, cutting 50m strips on alternate banks or cutting banks on alternate years. This is all about not removing habitat, which is both food and shelter for these bundles of fluff.

There is also another invasive species that can cause trouble for water voles. The American, or signal, crayfish has colonised vast amounts of the UK's waterways, outcompeting our native crayfish in the process.

The trouble they cause is exacerbated by the deeper and bigger tunnels these aliens dig into the riverbanks, undermining their integrity and causing them to slump into the water. This, in turn, requires the authorities or landowners to step in to repair the damage. Too much slumping can result in channels becoming impossibly narrow, thereby reducing their value for both wildlife and the many people who sail, row, paddle and swim. In fact, the crayfish alone are not so bad; rather it is the twin effect of their holes combined with motorised river boats who ignore the rules and travel too fast, creating a wake that splashes into the holes, and undermines the bank. There is actually a positive side to these aliens; water voles are particularly fond of eating the crayfish.

When banks need to be repaired the obvious problem is how to accommodate water voles, as most repairs in the last 60 years or so have been done using concrete or metal. Again, more sympathetic options are available. Willow poles driven into the river bottom and woven with withies (living willow branches) create an organic fence that will allow water voles to access the bank. And there is a growing interest in coconuts! Well, not the nuts themselves but the fibre, coir, which can be pre-planted with species such as lesser pond sedge, purple loosestrife, yellow flag iris, reed canary grass and soft rush and then rolled along the bank. When secured in place it helps reduce erosion without removing water vole habitat.

One of the best ways to improve the lot of the water vole is to look to its much bigger cousin the beaver. Beavers were driven to extinction in the UK in the late 18th century, after centuries of persecution. However, a more enlightened approach to wildlife is being seen in some quarters, allowing for the return of this amazing animal, and it is now firmly reestablished along our waterways. Research has repeatedly shown that when beaver are reintroduced into the landscape, other wildlife benefits massively, especially the water vole.

This is, obviously, a very abbreviated look at what can be done to help improve the habitat of the water vole. There are ecological consultants and Wildlife Trusts around the country who are able to offer the support that landowners need to serve our voles.

So what comes next? When the mink have gone and the riparian habitat has been repaired it is possible to think about releasing a new starter population of water voles. This in itself requires careful consideration: how many should be released and into what area? At the heart of this is the concept of the minimum viable population (MVP), which is the smallest isolated population with a good chance of surviving for a decent amount of time. One male water vole on a beautiful island of voley goodness would obviously not be a viable population; likewise, a million of them on a desert island would not work either. The MVP is a point between these two absurd extremes and the islands in this case are not as absolute as one in the middle of the Atlantic. These can be islands created by busy roads, housing developments or industrially produced crops.

> Rivers are not purely simple lines in the countryside, they are meandering beings that help create a mosaic of wetland habitats.

For water voles the requirements are thought to be in excess of 100 individuals at peak breeding season, which would mean around 30-50 at the start of the breeding season, occupying around 1.5-2km of good habitat. Unsurprisingly, the more voles and the larger the habitat, the better the chances of this population surviving.

Tying this in with other parts of a metapopulation will also increase the chances of survival, but this means that the work to repair the habitat must also extend to ensuring connectivity.

The only way to get water voles back into our landscape is to work across all of the problems they face. Mink need to be eradicated from the entire river catchment into which voles are to be released, but that alone is not enough. Rivers are not purely simple lines in the countryside, they are meandering beings that help create a mosaic of wetland habitats. The practice of tidying up rivers needs to be tamed, rivers need to be allowed to express a bit of will, to become a little wilder. Livestock needs to be kept back from the water's edge to stop cattle breaking down the banks, disturbing or destroying water vole nests. Furthermore, until beavers are more common, coppicing in the riparian habitat will generate a far more diverse and abundant ecosystem, benefiting not just water voles but a whole host of other waterside wildlife.

Once a site has been prepared and considered suitable for a vole injection, the translocation gets under way. Again, the team at Coombeshead have developed an efficient system. Voles are not just tipped out into the wild, they have what is known as a soft release. Six siblings per box are taken to the release point and then placed in a special pen in which they are fed for four days before a board is lifted at the front, revealing two vole-sized holes. For the next two days food is placed in the box, and while some voles may just up and go, others use this time to further fatten up and familiarise themselves with their new patch. Their shelter is then removed and they head off to fulfil their mission – completing this brilliant bit of conservation work by making new homes and new babies.

People's Trust for Endangered Species

People's Trust for Endangered Species (PTES) has been involved in water vole conservation for many years and sits on the UK Water Vole Steering Group. Since 1997, PTES has funded 46 water vole projects. We have investigated what provides safe refuge for water voles from American mink. We discovered the best ways to restore good bankside habitat and we have recently studied the effects of waterway maintenance on local populations of water voles. Working with many other people nationwide, we're doing the best we can to save this species from extinction. We know what needs to be done, but we need to monitor our progress properly to be sure of success and to act where it's needed.

National Water Vole Monitoring Programme

To ensure that we have a better picture of what's happening to the species nationally and that we're in a position to act quickly when needed, PTES launched the first ongoing National Water Vole Monitoring Programme (NWVMP). Covering England, Scotland and Wales, the NVWMP, established in 2015, works in collaboration with The Wildlife Trusts, Natural Resources Wales, Scottish Natural Heritage, Environment Agency, Natural England and RSPB. The NWVMP aims to bring together all current monitoring, as well as resurvey sites from previous national surveys.

National Surveys

The Vincent Wildlife Trust conducted two national surveys between 1989-90 and 1996-98 (carried out by Rob Strachan) that first demonstrated the dramatic decline of water voles across Britain. The sites that were visited during these two surveys form the basis of the National Water Vole Monitoring Programme. By regularly resurveying these sites, PTES can identify any changes that have happened since the late 1990s, as well as detect any emerging national trends.

Initial signs from the monitoring programme give us some cause for hope, but there's much more to be done if we are to better understand the threats facing Britain's water voles and help to protect them.

How to take part

You don't need to be an expert to get involved in the monitoring programme, anyone can register to take part, you just need to be willing to learn what to look out for. As with many mammals, it's not always possible to see water voles even if they are present, so often the best way of confirming their presence is to keep an eye out for signs they have left behind. These include their droppings (usually left in piles called latrines), feeding signs/remains and burrows in the bankside (or in certain habitats, nests).

We ask volunteers to survey one 500m length of riverbank at an allocated site once a year, usually between 15th April and 15th June. You will record all water vole field signs that you see, along with any otter and mink field signs to gain an insight into the distribution of these two species. A survey pack, including clear instructions on how to do your survey and a field signs ID guide, is provided.

If you already record water voles, you can register your site and add your data to the survey.

To find out more about taking part please visit www.ptes.org/watervoles.

Helping Water Voles on Your Land

Landowners are particularly well placed to help water voles, by creating and maintaining the optimum habitat they need to thrive. In 2019 PTES produced a 'Helping water voles on your land' guide for the wider farming community and landowners, highlighting management actions that are water vole friendly.

The guide offers advice on simple improvements to land management practices that can enhance the suitability of habitat for water voles, helping to connect colonies across the countryside. The four main areas covered include: management beside water courses; buffer strips; sympathetic water-course and ditch management; and restoring recreating and managing wetland habitats.

The guide describes the benefits of these actions to water voles, as well as other native wildlife – from amphibians to invertebrates. Control of non-native American mink is also covered, in addition to details about agrienvironmental schemes. The guide is endorsed by the UK Water Vole Steering group, which includes representatives of the following organisations: Environment Agency, Natural England, Natural Resources Wales, Scottish Natural Heritage, People's Trust for Endangered Species, Royal Society for the Protection of Birds and The Wildlife Trusts.

To download a free copy of the guide, visit www.ptes.org/water-voles.

Water Vole by Jen Tetlow.

Myths, Art and Literature

Myths and Legends

As the water vole is usually a small, discreet mammal, they have not entered the canon of myth and legend to any great extent. They do make an appearance, but not always with the same sort of affection as seen in *The Wind in the Willows*.

George Sim, in his 1903 volume *The Vertebrate Fauna of Dee*, writes, 'This species has been brought to me under the name of "Earth Hound," a mythical animal supposed by the rural population of Aberdeen and Banff shires to frequent graveyards, making its way through coffins and devouring the dead. Of course, no proof was ever forthcoming that these ravages had taken place, and how such ideas should have arise it is impossible to explain.' Interestingly, Sim does note that there were thought to be two species of water vole, brown and black, but that they are now recognised as identical.

It is possible that the fossorial voles of Glasgow are of a similar temperament as those that had received such unwarranted accusations – making burrows in a graveyard is always going to be considered untoward!

Perhaps guided by a similar mistrust, the lavellan was a rodent, larger than a rat, from northern Scotland that lived in water, and which had the power to poison cattle over 100 feet away. However, the preserved skin of this animal was also able to impart healing properties to water into which it had been dipped. The name in Scottish Gaelic, *làbhallan*, is used for both water vole and water shrew.

Definitely making it into the territory of myth is the story told about Viscount Montgomery of Alamein – Monty – who was notorious for his lack of tact. In the book *The Lonely Leader*, Alistair

Home writes, 'there is the widely told story about ex-Sergeant Parker who stayed on at Islington Mill as odd-job man during the last years of the Field Marshal. The unfortunate Parker was said to have been attacked by a horde of infuriated water-rats while clearing weed out of the mill-race and died as a result of his injuries. "Most unfortunate" was supposed to have been Monty's callous comment.' The fact that the story is so ridiculous yet has had the legs to last is a testament to the nature of the man, however, it is also completely untrue.

Though to judge by this headline in the *Daily Mail*, you might be forgiven for thinking otherwise: 'The water vole inspired one of Wind in the Willows best loved characters, but in real life they are as vicious as they are cunning'. In defence of that paper, this was taken from an interview with the ecologist and author Tom Moorhouse, more of whom later.

In the 1800s there was an angler's bait made from a cork called 'the water vole', which was aimed at catching pike. There are still baits bearing the same name around today. Typically it floats on the water in the wake of a boat and has a long tail that moves in the water. It is a vicious piece of kit with two grappling-type hooks suspended underneath and is specifically for catching very large bass.

In the past, the Catholic Church decreed that riparian mammals (those living in very close proximity to water) were fish and could thus be eaten on fast days when meat was forbidden.

Art and Literature

The Wind in the Willows by Kenneth Grahame

The obvious place to start has to be the magical tale of *The Wind in the Willows*. Or maybe not obvious if you are struggling with more archaic names for this rodent. Water voles were often referred to as water rats, and in Grahame's epic story, we have Ratty, the water vole.

Ratty is introduced to the story by Mole, and while guide books may be more scientific and photographs ever-so revealing, there is no mistaking who we are meeting in this description.

'As he sat on the grass and looked across the river, a dark hole in the bank opposite, just above the water's edge, caught his eye, and dreamily he fell to considering what a nice snug dwelling-place it would make for an animal with few wants and fond of a bijou riverside residence, above flood level and remote from noise and dust.

As he gazed, something bright and small seemed to twinkle down in the heart of it, vanished, then twinkled once more like a tiny star. But it could hardly be a star in such an unlikely situation; and it was too glittering and small for a glow-worm. Then, as he looked, it winked at him, and so declared itself to be an eye; and a small face began gradually to grow up round it, like a frame round a picture.

A brown little face with whiskers.

A grave round face, with the same twinkle in its eye that had first attracted his notice.

Small neat ears and thick silky hair.

It was the Water Rat!'

The Wind in the Willows began life as a sequence of bedtime stories for Kenneth Grahame's son before it was finally published in 1908. The adventures feature a principal quartet of Rat, Mole, Toad and Badger, with a host of other characters appearing along the way. The writing is wonderfully evocative of the English countryside and starts with the spring and summer that Ratty and Mole spend together before they come across the boastful Mr Toad in his hall. Many of us will also be familiar with the version of the story that was dramatised by A. A. Milne, of Winnie the Pooh fame, Toad of Toad Hall.

The serially enthusiastic Toad takes the friends on a romp in his latest obsession, the horse-drawn caravan, until he has his head turned when the caravan is wrecked by an automobile. His car craze leads to escalating collisions and the equally escalating concern of Rat and Mole, who seek council from wise Badger of the Wild Wood.

The three mammals attempt an intervention, but Toad ignores the guidance of his friends and escapes, stealing an unattended car. Capture and prison threaten to end his adventures until the jailer's daughter takes pity on the anthropomorphic amphibian, who is eventually rescued from further drama by reliable Rat.

In what might be a plot spoiler, that rescue leads into the final drama as Toad is informed that his beloved Toad Hall has been overrun by lesser mustelids: stoats, weasels and ferrets. Thankfully, Badger knows of a secret tunnel which allows the four friends to gain access, win a decisive battle, evict those Wild Wooders and organise a banquet.

Above: The raid on Toad Hall from *The Wind in the Willows*, with a gun-toting Ratty on the left.

The romp of this part of the tale is what we have become familiar with, but perhaps what is forgotten are the moments of almost psychedelic whimsy that Grahame brings to the book. In the chapter titled 'The Piper at the Gates of Dawn', Rat and Mole have an adventure which turns so mystical that it is easy to see where Pink Floyd got inspiration for their 1967 album of the same name. There is a phrase within that chapter which perfectly captures the state of grief that comes from the growing awareness of the loss of nature, 'they stared blankly, in dumb misery deepening as they slowly realised all they had seen and all they had lost...'

The two friends are then comforted, not by a solution but by 'the gift of forgetfulness. Lest the awful remembrance should remain and grow, and overshadow mirth and pleasure, and the great haunting memory should spoil all the after-lives of little animals helped out of difficulties, in order that they should be happy and light-hearted as before.' This is a book that is far more than a children's story, and the fact that it features a water vole is just a great bonus.

In the chapter 'Wayfarers All', Rat gets schooled in migration by the restive swallows. When they tell him of the wonders of their southern home he asks why they ever come back to this 'poor drab little country?' The swallow responds by describing the call (yes, there is a call) to head north. 'The call of lush meadow-grass, wet orchards, warm, insect-haunted ponds, of browsing cattle, of haymaking, and all the farm buildings clustered rough the House of the perfect Eaves?' One wonders how Kenneth Grahame would look upon our despoiled farmland now?

The thought of adventure has entered Rat's mind and, as he sits and ponders the limitations of his life, he is met by a wayfarer, a seafaring rat who tells such tales of adventure; of sea journeys, of the cities of the Mediterranean, and of the scents and sounds of a different world, and tells them with such power that Ratty becomes determined to leave his gentle existence behind. The sea rat tells him, ''Tis but a banging of the door behind you, a blithesome step forward, and you are out of the old life and into the new!'

It is only the intervention of Mole, who finds our Ratty ready with stout stick and full satchel about to hit the road south, that the world returns to order.

A work like this has not escaped deeper analysis. By many, Mole is identified as the author, Rat as a representative of the comfortable middle class, Badger as the gatekeeper between the middle class and the working class rabble, the Wild Wooders, who rise up against the repulsive hyper consumption of the *nouveau riche* Toad. Though in this story, the plucky establishment is able to return things to their proper order. How different this book might have been had it been written after 1917 and the Russian Revolution?

Books by Tom Moorhouse

It is surprising that a small rat-sized rodent should attract the level of literary attention as it does. Not only does Kenneth Grahame gift the water vole a central role in one of the all-time great books, but zoologist Tom Moorhouse has stepped in to pick up the mantle and create his own re-vole-utionary universe. Starting with *The River Singers*, Moorhouse introduces us to the wonderful world of Sylvan and his siblings as they find their lives turned upside down with the arrival of a mink onto their stretch of the river.

While Graeme might have the edge with luminous prose, Moorhouse steals a march on the master with stories that not only grip you into a page-turning, not-going-to-sleep-until-I-finish frenzy, but are also full of zoological and ecological facts. It is never didactic; the facts subtly slip into the narrative as you enjoy the romp.

An indication of the quality of *The River Singers* and its sequel, *The Rising*, is that the Grahame estate gave Tom permission to write a sequence called *The New Adventures of Mr Toad*. Similar characters return in these illustrated books including, of course, Ratty, described by Tom as a 'Helpful chap, but included to chafe his elders. Still lives in same old riverbank property (small, somewhat damp, suitable for Water Rats and the like), I believe inherited by seafaring relations of Dear Old Ratty.'

Questing Vole by Dru Marland.

Water Vole by Kate Wyatt.

Since then, Moorhouse has written a more serious, though in places brilliantly funny, account of life as a water vole ecologist. *Elegy for a River* is full of information that will enthuse a few into life as a field ecologist, and certainly put some off as well! It is from this book that we learn of the ability of this bundle of fluff to be full of vicious cunning, but one of its delights is the window it also opens into the real world of ecological fieldwork, in particular the vagaries of doing such work in the UK working on a small mammal. There are ecologists out there who get to watch elephants in Africa and then there are ecologists who get to fall into cold rivers and slosh home in water-filled waders.

There is a rather glancing reference to the water vole in Evelyn Waugh's satire *Scoop*. So famous is the phrase that it has become a cornerstone in the teaching of nature writing... as how NOT to do it! William Boot notes, in his nature notes column of the *Daily Beast*, 'Feather footed through the plashy fen passes the questing vole.' Purple prose – so easy to get carried away!

'Bertram tried swimming because everyone said he should like it, being a water vole, and his mum said you should always try everything at least once.'

Bertram Learns to Sew
by Karin Celestine

One of Karin Celestine's delightful books for children, *Bertram Learns to Sew* features Bertram, a water vole who does not really like swimming and enjoys sewing instead. He has swimming lessons but finds his true place in water vole society by sewing and repairing his family's clothes. A heartwarming tale about being 'different' and following your passion in life.

Dear Bertram
Always try everything at least once.
Eat well and keep sewing.
Lots of Love
Mum
xxx

Bertram Vole
The Garden Pond
The Shed
Wales

Ophelia by Sir John Everett Millais.

Ophelia by John Everett Millais

Artistic representations of the water vole, beyond those that appear with varying degrees of reality in the natural history volumes of the ages, are few and far between. Perhaps the most thrilling one is, unfortunately, invisible!

The wonderful writer Amy-Jane Beer writes about this vole in her new book, *The Flow: Rivers Water and Wildness*. This hidden vole has high artistic pretensions with a deep connection to both the Pre-Raphaelite Brotherhood and Shakespeare. John Everett Millais' most famous painting is that of *Ophelia*, floating lifeless in a stream, surrounded by flowers and water weed. It is a stunningly beautiful work, based on many hours of study of Hogsmill River in Surrey and many hours of suffering by the muse of the day, Elizabeth Siddall, who had to lie in a bath of water on many occasions, including the time the heating lamps went out and Siddall became so chilled she needed medical attention. While it is much loved now and on permanent display in the Tate, it was not universally adored on its unveiling, *The Times* wrote, 'there must be something strangely perverse in an imagination which souses Ophelia in a weedy ditch, and robs the drowning struggle of the lovelorn maiden of all pathos and beauty.'

Where is the vole? You can stare at the picture as long as you like, playing a version of Pre-Raphaelite *Where's Wally* perhaps. But you won't see it. In 1851, when the picture was first exhibited to friends, no one could work out what the small creature swimming next to the floating girl was supposed to be. Guesses were made, a hare was suggested, but the reaction of Millais suggested not, so more came.

A rabbit, or maybe a dog or cat? This was enough to convince the artist to remove the rodent – a great loss for those interested in the iconography of the water vole, but just possibly this was what allowed *Ophelia* to become such a revered painting.

It is unlikely Millais had the intention of making such a pertinent point with his vole erasure, but if we don't work hard at keeping Ratty in his home then future generations may end up wondering what was once there when looking at the waterways of this country.

It is entirely possible that if we do nothing more to help the water voles, they will become extinct in Britain. What an utterly appalling event that would be, a humble icon that has found its way into the hearts of millions no longer being there to entrance our children and their children too.

We have to make sure that does not happen, so look to your local patch and check whether there are water voles; if there are, fight to keep them healthy, and if not, work with local wildlife groups to find a way of getting them back. Britain would be a much lesser place without the water vole.

Water Vole and Mistletoe by Kate Wyatt.

Water Vole by Archibald Thorburn.

Water Vole by Jane Russ.

Photo credits and artworks

Myths, Art and Literature

Jen Tetlow: page 134.
Public domain: pages 139, 140, 142, 154.
Dru Marland: page 145.
Kate Wyatt: pages 146, 153.
Karin Celestine: pages 148, 149.
Alamy: page 150.

Endpaper linocuts and page 155 by Jane Russ.

Every effort has been made to trace copyright holders of material and acknowledge permission for this publication. The publisher apologises for any errors or omissions to rights holders and would be grateful for notification of credits and corrections that should be included in future reprints or editions of this book.

Acknowledgements

This book has only been possible thanks to the work done by amazing naturalists who have been happy to share their experiences with me.

Kate Long was the first to persuade me of their special nature while I was researching my book, *The Beauty in the Beast*. Jo Cartmell, Pete Cooper, Tom Moorehouse, Merely Gelling and, of course, Derek Gow and his team at Rewildling Combeshead have such a deep knowledge about this amazing animal.

More than ever, series editor Jane Russ has been instrumental in helping pull this book together, thank you.

Photographers continue to amaze me with their dedication – thank you all for allowing your brilliant work to illustrate this book.

And a special thank you to Kenneth Grahame – re-reading *The Wind in the Willows* was a treat, and if I had not been writing this book, it would not have happened.

Books in the series

www.graffeg.com

The Water Vole Book
Published in Great Britain in 2023 by Graffeg
Limited.

Written by Hugh Warwick copyright © 2023.
Designed and produced by Graffeg Limited
copyright © 2023. Series editor Jane Russ.

Graffeg Limited, 24 Stradey Park Business
Centre, Mwrwg Road, Llangennech, Llanelli,
Carmarthenshire, SA14 8YP, Wales, UK.
Tel: 01554 824000. www.graffeg.com.

A CIP Catalogue record for this book is
available from the British Library.

The publisher gratefully acknowledges the
financial support of this book by the Books
Council of Wales. www.gwales.com.

Printed in China TT211122

ISBN 9781802581676

1 2 3 4 5 6 7 8 9